SWIMMING TIME!

by Brendan Flynn

BUMBA BOOKS™

LERNER PUBLICATIONS ◆ MINNEAPOLIS

Note to Educators:

Throughout this book, you'll find critical thinking questions. These can be used to engage young readers in thinking critically about the topic and in using the text and photos to do so.

Lerner Publications Company
A division of Lerner Publishing Group, Inc.
241 First Avenue North
Minneapolis, MN 55401 USA

For reading levels and more information, look up this title at www.lernerbooks.com.

Library of Congress Cataloging-in-Publication Data

The Cataloging-in-Publication Data for *Swimming Time!* is on file at the Library of Congress.
ISBN 978-1-5124-1435-6 (lib. bdg.)
ISBN 978-1-5124-1545-2 (pbk.)
ISBN 978-1-5124-1546-9 (EB pdf)

Manufactured in the United States of America
1 – VP – 7/15/16

LERNER

SOURCE

Expand learning beyond the printed book. Download free, complementary educational resources for this book from our website, www.lerneresource.com.

Table of Contents

We Swim

Swimming is fun.

You can swim alone.

Or swimming can be a team sport.

You do not need much

to swim.

You need a pool.

You need a swimsuit.

Some people

wear goggles.

Many pools are indoors.

A pool has lanes.

Each swimmer stays in a lane.

You dive into the pool.

Then you swim to the other end.

Swimmers race against each other.

Why might swimmers dive into a pool?

You swim to the end
of the pool and back.
That is called a lap.
Some races last
many laps.

You use different strokes

in different races.

You face forward for most strokes.

Sometimes you swim on your back.

15

Judges time

the swimmers.

The fastest swimmer is

the winner.

How do the judges time the swimmers?

You can see a swim meet
at your school.

Or you can watch one on TV.

**Where else
might you see
people swimming?**

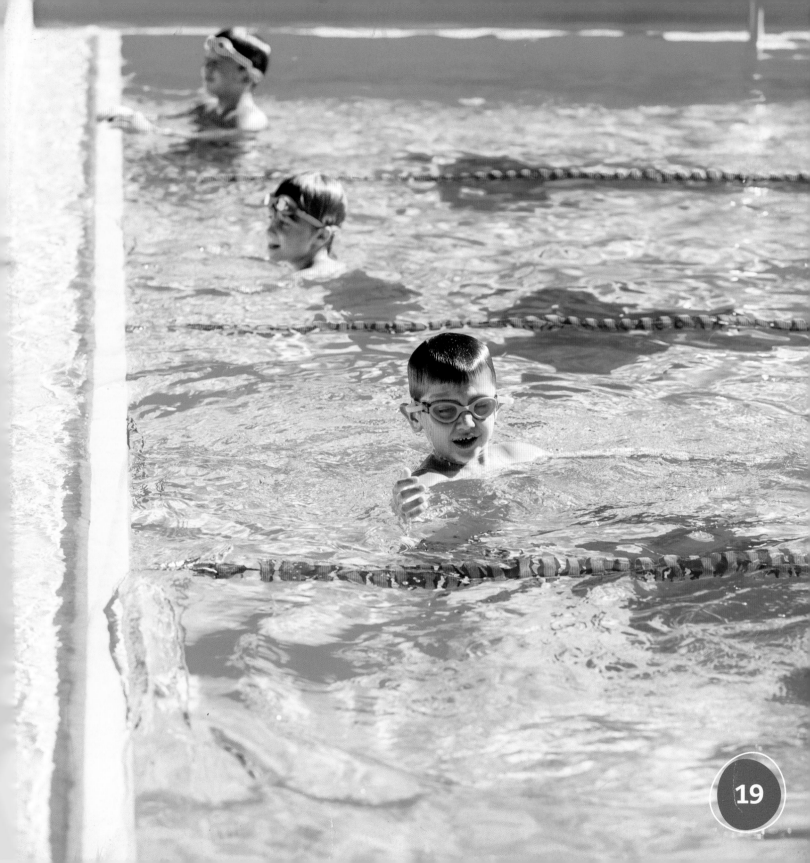

Swimming is great exercise.

It is a fun sport!

Swimming Pool

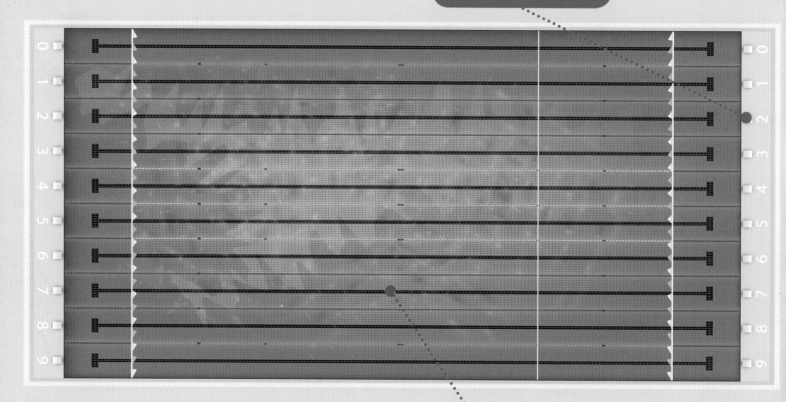

starting block

lane

Picture Glossary

dive

to jump into the water head first

lanes

areas that a swimmer stays in

lap

to swim to one end of the pool and back

strokes

certain ways of swimming

23

Index

Read More

Gifford, Clive. *Swimming and Diving.* Mankato, MN: Amicus, 2012.

Nelson, Robin. *Swimming Is Fun!* Minneapolis: Lerner Publications, 2014.

Tieck, Sarah. *Swimming.* Minneapolis: Abdo Publishing, 2013.

Photo Credits